AF271001

Level PreK/K

Lesley Mandel Morrow
Senior Author

Program Consultants

Sarah Sprinkel
Early Childhood/Community Outreach
Senior Director
Orange County Public Schools
Orlando, Florida

Rosita Saloun
Director, Early Childhood Education
Community School District Six
New York, New York

Donna A. Shadle
Principal
St. Mary Elementary and Preschool
Massillon, Ohio

Helen Wood Turner, Ed.D.
Deputy Director of Education
Associates for Renewal in Education, Inc.
Washington, D.C.

Regina Connaughton Mohan
Coordinator, Early Childhood Program
Visitation Academy
Brooklyn, New York

Carol S. Gannon, Ed.D.
Director of Pupil Personnel Services
Port Washington UFSD
Port Washington, New York

Sr. Colleen Dougherty, IHM M.Ed.
Director, Day Care-Preschool Center
St. Monica School
Philadelphia, Pennsylvania

Celeste Smith
Pre-School Director/Teacher
St. John Vianney School
Orlando, Florida

Sadlier-Oxford
A Division of William H. Sadlier, Inc.
New York, New York 10005-1002

Advisors

Special thanks to the following teachers and Rutgers University School of Education graduate students who reviewed portions of the initial manuscript for the author, Lesley Mandel Morrow:

Jennifer Castro
Pre-Kindergarten Teacher
Lincoln School
New Brunswick, New Jersey

Dana Mitchell Walker
Kindergarten Teacher
Clinton School
Plainfield, New Jersey

Joanne Palacino
Pre-Kindergarten Teacher
P.S. 173/ D.O. 6
New York, New York

Deborah Woo
Tutoring Program Coordinator
New Brunswick, New Jersey

Phyllis Thomson
Pre-Kindergarten Teacher
Lincoln School
New Brunswick, New Jersey

Product Development and Management: Leslie A. Baranowski

Photo Credits

Animals Animals/William D. Griffin: 51 bottom right.
Janette Beckman: 19 bottom right, 41.
Cate Photography: 37, 38.
Bruce Coleman/ Nasha Nordbye: 67 bottom right.
FPG International/ Richard Price: 24 bottom right.
The Image Bank/ Luis Castenada: 67 top right.
International Stock/ Andre Jenny: 35; John Michael: 67 top left.
Nawrocki Stock Photo/ Mauritius: 54 bottom.

The Stock Market/Gay Bumgarner: 51 top right; Zefa Germany: 53 top.
Superstock: 67 bottom left.
Tony Stone Images/ Timothy Shonnard: 24 top right; R.B. Studio: 24 top left; Nello Giambi: 51 top left; Mitch York: 24 bottom left.
Visuals Unlimited/ Kjell B. Sandved: 51 bottom left, 53 bottom; A. Kerstitch: 54 top.

Illustrators

Dirk Wunderlich: Cover Art
Leo Abbett: 8
Rose Berlin: 9,66
Terri and Joe Chicko: 13, 14, 39, 45, 77
Cameron Eagle: 41
Dagmar Fehlau: 5, 6,18, 21, 22, 73
Laura Freeman: 7
Dave Garbot: 32, 62, 68
Myron Grossman: 36, 52, 77
Tim Haggerty: 15, 59, 61, 79
Steve Henry: 16, 40, 49, 60
Dave Jonason: 10, 20, 48

Terry Kovalcik: 11, 50
Andy Levine: 17, 29, 31, 44, 46, 73
Jason Levinson: 47
Tammy Lyons: 57, 63
Ben Mahan: 23, 28, 30, 33, 34, 43, 64
Winifred Barnum-Neuman: 12
Laura Rader: 55, 56, 79
BB Sams: 26, 58, 65, 69, 70, 75
Ellen Joy Sasaki: 25, 27
Lorianne Siomades: 42
Terry Taylor: Mother Goose Logos

ZB Font Method Copyright © 1996 Zaner-Bloser

Copyright © 2001 by William H. Sadlier, Inc. All rights reserved.

This publication, or any part thereof, may not be reproduced in any form, or by any means, including electronic, photographic, or mechanical, or by any sound recording system, or by any device for storage and retrieval of information, without the written permission of the publisher. Address inquiries to Permissions Department, William H. Sadlier, Inc., 9 Pine Street, New York, New York 10005-1002.

𝕊 is a registered trademark of William H. Sadlier, Inc.

Printed in the United States of America

ISBN: 0-8215-6950-3
  3456789/03 02 01 00

Contents

Copyright © 2001 by William H. Sadlier, Inc. All rights reserved.

Star Light

Star light,
Star bright,
First star
I see tonight,
I wish I may,
I wish I might,
Have this wish
I wish tonight.

© William H. Sadlier, Inc. All rights reserved.

Think and Share
What will you wish for when you see a star?

Purposes: Phonemic Awareness—Rhyme; Reading Behavior—Responding to Text
Directions: Look at the picture as I read the rhyme aloud. Now look at the words as I read the rhyme aloud.

Home Activity

Dear Family,

Read the rhyme "Star Light" on the reverse side of this page to your child. Talk with your child about his or her bedtime routine.

Directions: Look at the pictures. Talk about what Bonnie Bunny does before she goes to sleep at night. Then help Bonnie get to bed. Have your child use a finger and then a crayon to follow the maze from Bonnie to her bed. To see a bedtime teddy bear, help your child fold back the page to make the arrow points touch at the top and bottom of the page.

Apreciada Familia:

Lea al niño la rima "Star Light" que se encuentra en la página 5. Hable con el niño acerca de su rutina a la hora de acostarse.

Indicaciones: Miren la foto. Hablen sobre lo que Bonnie Bunny hace todas las noches antes de ir a dormir. Después ayude a Bonnie a acostarse. Pida al niño usar un dedo y un lápiz de cera para seguir el laberinto que lleva a Bonnie a su cama. Para ayudar a su niño a ver un osito, ayúdelo a doblar la página haciendo coincidir los puntos de las flechas que se encuentran arriba y abajo de la página.

6

Purpose: Oral Language Development—Communicating Personal Experiences

Visit us at
www.sadlier-oxford.com

© William H. Sadlier, Inc. All rights reserved.

Purpose: Oral Language Development—Building Vocabulary

Directions: Mom and Jen are camping out in their backyard. There are a lot of animals still awake. I see an owl. What other animals do you see? Point to and name each animal.

Purpose: Phonemic Awareness and Auditory Discrimination—
Environmental Sounds

Materials: "Brother John" in the Teacher's Resource Guide
(page T38) and recording on CD and Theme 1 cassette

Directions: Listen to the song. Look at the picture. What makes the
sound "ring, ring, ring"? Circle it. What makes the sound "ruff, ruff,
ruff"? Circle it. What makes the sound "waa, waa, waa"? Circle it.

Home Activity

Talk with your child
about sounds that wake
both of you up in the
morning. Take turns
making the sounds.

8

Activity 3

© William H. Sadlier, Inc. All rights reserved.

Time to Listen

Purpose: Listening Comprehension—Recalling Details
Materials: "Teddy Bear, Teddy Bear" in the Teacher's Resource Guide (page T38) and recording on CD and Theme 1 cassette
Directions: Listen as I read the rhyme about teddy bear. Listen as I read the rhyme again. Look at the picture and color teddy bear's slippers the right color. Circle what teddy bear drinks. Tell what teddy bear turns off.

9

Activity 4

Purposes: Math—Recognizing Shapes; Building Vocabulary—Naming Shapes

Directions: Look at the sun. The shape of the sun is a circle. Talk about other things on the page that are circle shapes. Trace the gray line around the sun to make a circle. Now you're going to use your circle in the Math Center. (See page 10 in the Teacher's Resource Guide for the Math Center activity.)

10

Activity 5

With your child, find objects in your home that are shaped like a circle, such as a plate or clock.

© William H. Sadlier, Inc. All rights reserved.

Purpose: Visual Discrimination—Recognizing Same/Different
Materials: Punchout Cards on page 73
Directions: Help Max find socks that are the same. Place all of the cards with the picture side down in the basket. Pull out two cards. If the pictures are the same, put them next to Max. If the pictures are different, place the cards back in the basket and try again.

Activity 6

Purpose: Visual Discrimination—Recognizing Same/Different

Directions: Look at the beds of the three bears. Point to Papa Bear's bed. Circle the tie that is different. Point to Mama Bear's bed. Circle the pillow that is different. Point to Baby Bear's bed. Circle the teddy bear that is different.

Home Activity

With your child, talk about how two stuffed animals or two socks are alike and how they are different.

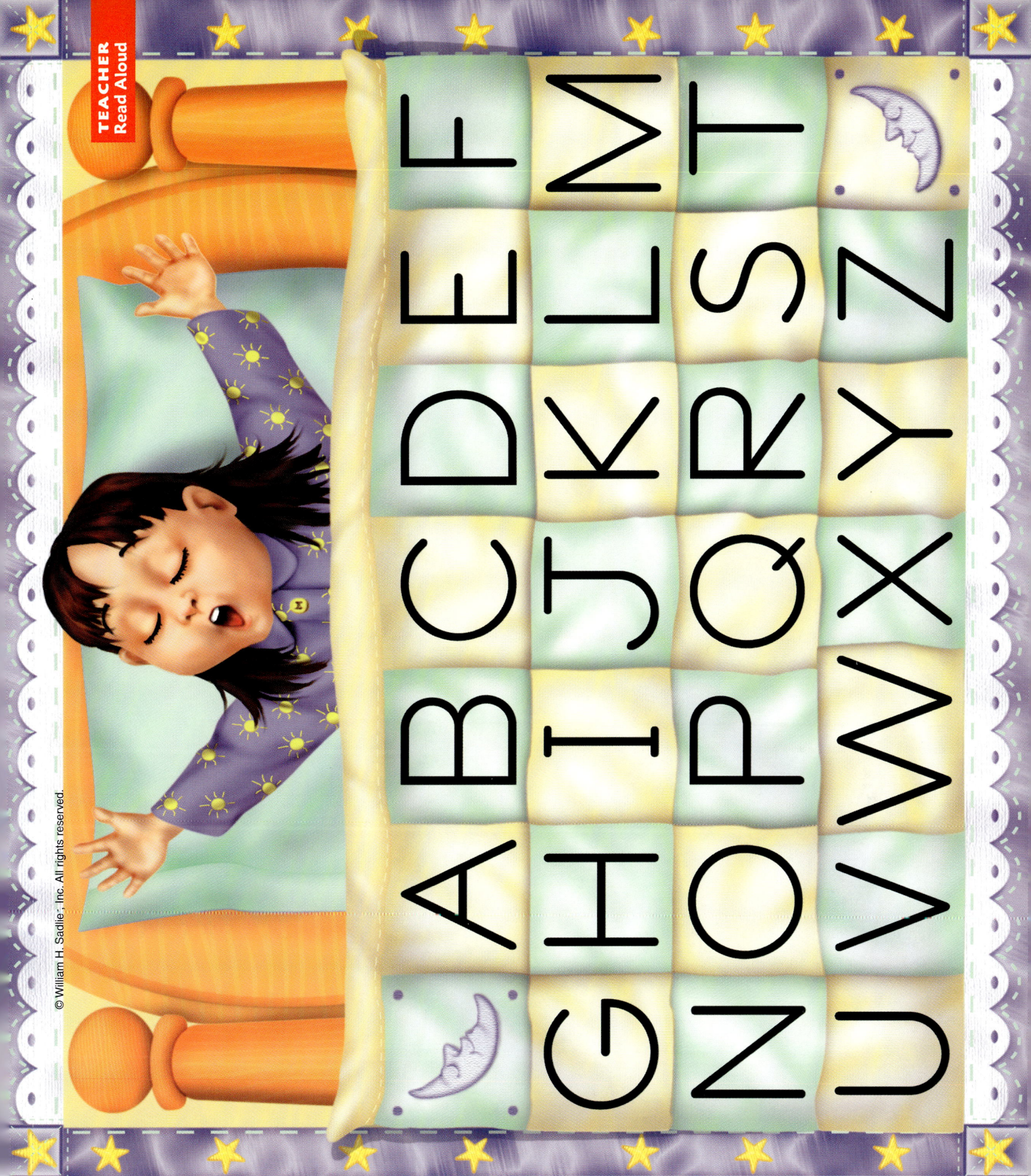

© William H. Sadlier, Inc. All rights reserved.

Purpose: Learning About the Alphabet—Recognizing Uppercase Letters
Materials: "The Good Morning, Good Night Alphabet Song" in the Teacher's Resource
Guide (page T38) and recording on CD and Theme 1 cassette
Directions: Point to each letter in the alphabet as I say its name. Now sing "The Good
Morning, Good Night Alphabet Song" with me. Circle the first letter in your name.

13

Activity 8

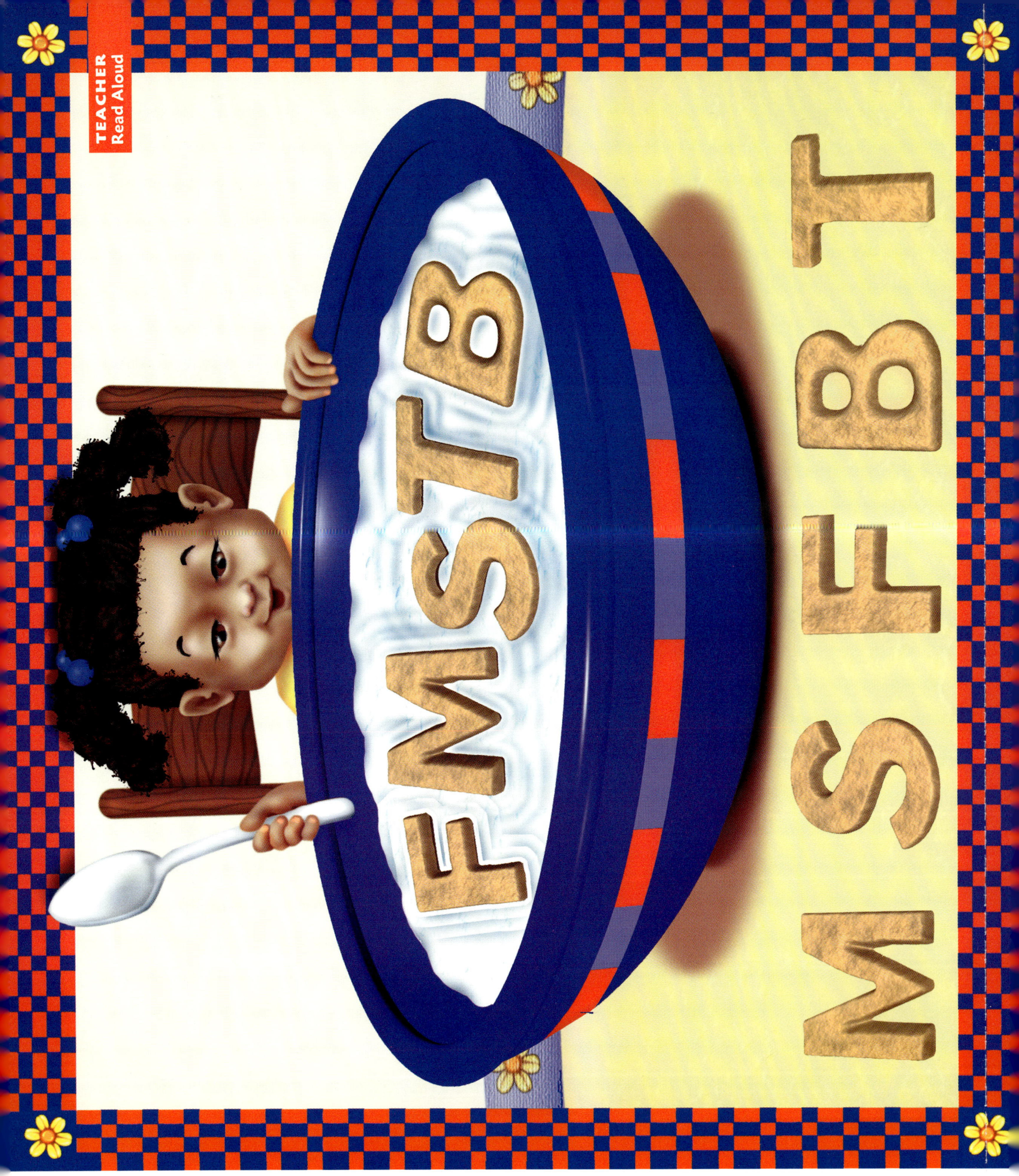

14

Purpose: Learning About the Alphabet—Recognizing and Matching Uppercase Letters

Directions: Janet is eating a bowl of alphabet cereal. Listen as I say a letter name. Point to the letter in the bowl with me. Then circle the same letter on the place mat.

Write uppercase letters on a piece of paper. Point to and name the letters. Have your child repeat them after you.

Tim   has   a   hat.

Tim   has   a   coat.

Tim   has   a   bag.

© William H. Sadlier, Inc. All rights reserved.

Purpose: Learning About Print—Demonstrating Left-to-Right Progression
Directions: Starting on the green dot, trace the dotted line with your finger as I read the words aloud.
Stop on the red dot. Listen as I read the words again and trace each dotted line with a crayon.

15

Activity 10

The pig is on the top.

The cow is on the bottom.

5

Purpose: Learning About Print—Demonstrating Top-to-Bottom Progression

Directions: When we read, we start at the top. Let's put our finger under the first word at the **top** of the page in the book. Listen as I read the words. Let's put our finger under the first word at the **bottom** of the page. Listen as I read the words. Go back and circle the words at the **top**. Then draw a line under the words at the **bottom**.

Home Activity

Have your child point to the top and bottom of a page in a book, newspaper, or magazine.

My Wish

© William H. Sadlier, Inc. All rights reserved.

Purpose: Learning About Print—Recognizing One's First Name
Directions: Inside the star, draw a picture of your wish. Then I will help you write your name on the line. Watch how we spell your name and write all the letters. Let's look at your name and read it together.

Activity 12

My Own Word Cards

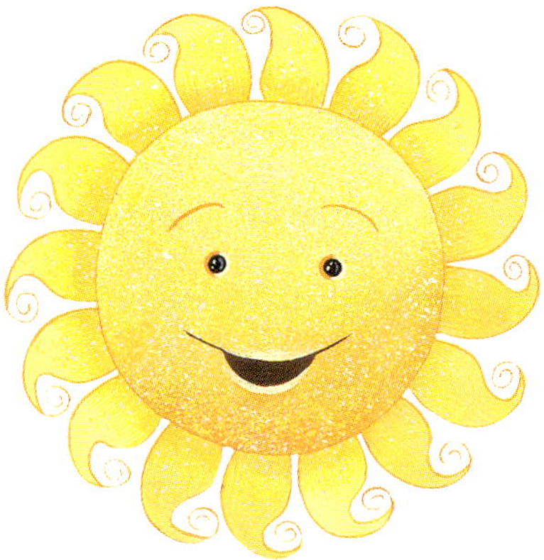

sun

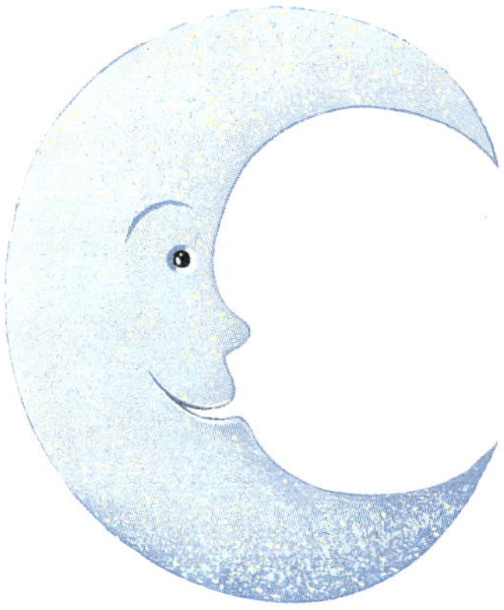

moon

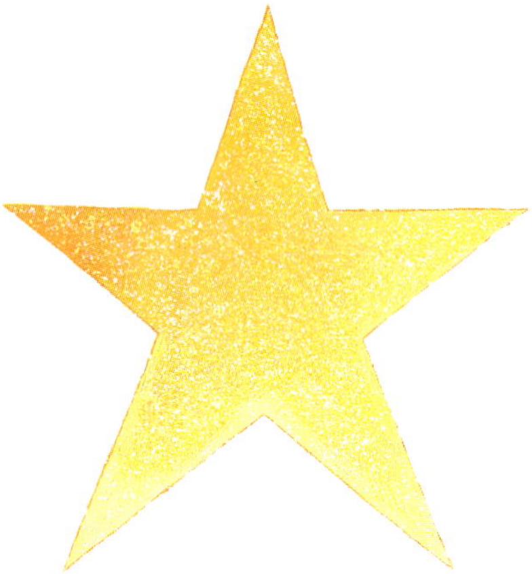

star

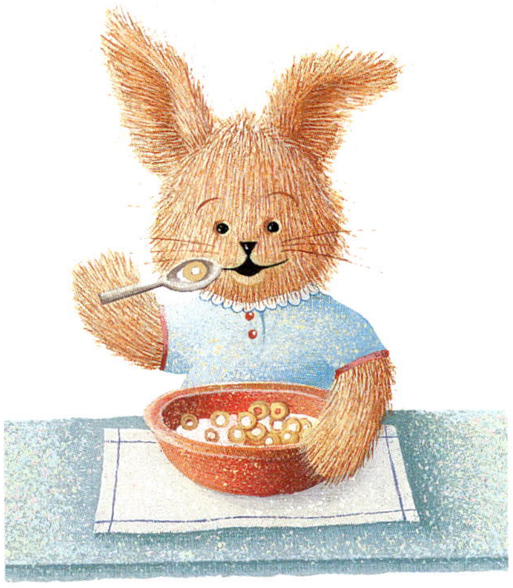

eat

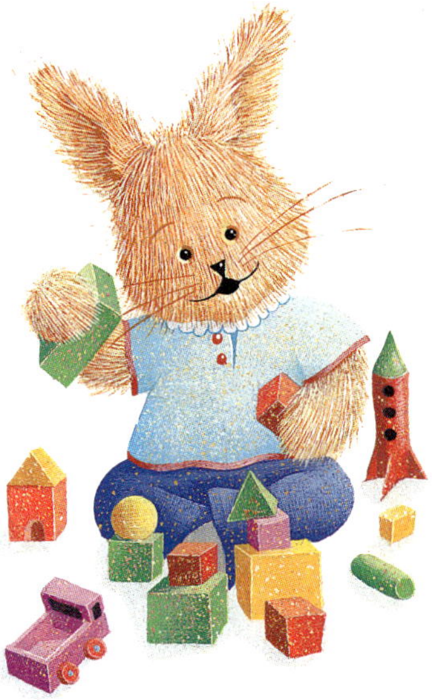

play

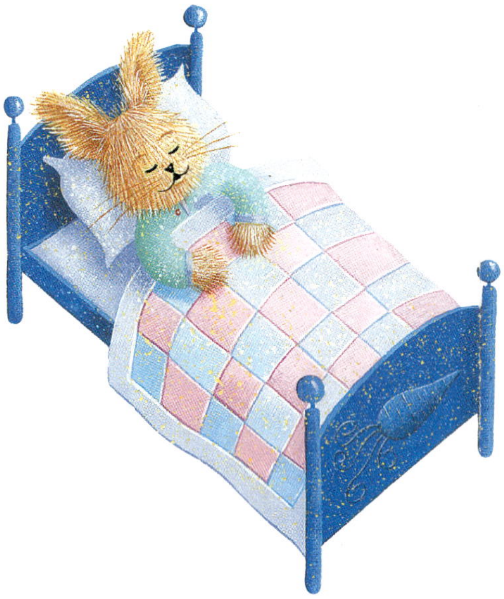

sleep

18

Purposes: Learning About Print—Recognizing Words; Sight Vocabulary—Theme Words
Directions: Let's talk about the pictures. What do you see? Listen as I read one of the words. Hold up the card with the picture and word I say.

Make a morning snack.

© William H. Sadlier, Inc. All rights reserved.

1. crackers

2. peanut butter

3. jelly

4. snack

Think and Share

What is your favorite morning snack?
How do you make it?

Purpose: Comprehension—Sequencing

Directions: Find out how to make a yummy morning snack. Point to each picture as I read about it. Now tell me how to make this snack.

Beginning to Write

20

Activity 15

Purpose: Writing—Sharing Ideas Through Drawing and Writing
Directions: Talk about foods you like to eat in the morning. Draw or write about your favorite breakfast food.

Ask your child to draw or write about a favorite family food.

![Bedtime for Bunny]

Bedtime for Bunny

★ 1

Directions: Have your child hold the book and turn the pages as you read the story aloud. After reading the story, ask your child to tell you what Bonnie Bunny did before she went to sleep.

Parent Read Aloud

Pajamas

Fold

Kiss!

★ 4

© William H. Sadlier, Inc. All rights reserved.

© William H. Sadlier, Inc. All rights reserved.

TAKE-HOME BOOK
Book Concepts: Knowing How to Hold a Book Upright;
Knowing How to Turn Pages Properly
Comprehension: Retelling a Story

21

Activity 16

2

Bear

Fold

Blanket

3

TAKE-HOME BOOK
Book Concepts: Knowing How to Hold a Book Upright;
Knowing How to Turn Pages Properly
Comprehension: Retelling a Story

Rain, Rain, Go Away

Rain,

Rain,

Go away;

Come again

Another day.

All the children

Want to play.

© William H. Sadlier, Inc. All rights reserved.

Think and Share
What do you like to do on rainy days?

Purposes: Phonemic Awareness—Rhyme;
Reading Behavior—Responding to Text
Directions: Look at the picture as I read the rhyme aloud.
Now look at the words as I read the rhyme aloud.

Home Activity

Dear Family,

Read the rhyme "Rain, Rain, Go Away" on the reverse side of this page to your child. Talk about fun things to do indoors on rainy days.

Directions: Look at the photos. Talk about activities you like to do outdoors on sunny, rainy, windy, and snowy days. Have your child ask other family members and friends the question, "What is your favorite kind of weather?" Help your child color in a box under the photo of the type of weather each person names. Then talk about the results of your weather survey.

Apreciada Familia:

Lea al niño la rima "Rain, Rain, Go Away" en la página 23. Hablen de las cosas amenas que se pueden hacer dentro de la casa durante un día de lluvia.

Indicaciones: Juntos miren las fotos. Hablen de las actividades que pueden hacer dentro de la casa durante un día de lluvia, un día soleado, ventoso o cuando está nevando. Pida al niño preguntar ¿cuál es tu tiempo favorito? a otros miembros y amigos de la familia. Ayúdelo a colorear un cuadro debajo de la foto del tipo de tiempo que cada persona escoja. Después hablen de los resultados de su encuesta sobre el tiempo.

Sunny

Rainy

Windy

Snowy

Purpose: Oral Language Development—Asking Questions

Visit us at
www.sadlier-oxford.com

© William H. Sadlier, Inc. All rights reserved.

Time
to
Talk

Purpose: Oral Language Development—Speaking in Complete Sentences
Directions: The family is trying on hats. I see a straw hat. This hat is for sunny days. Talk about a hat you see. Remember to use a complete sentence when you share your answer.

25

Activity 18

Purpose: Phonemic Awareness and Auditory Discrimination—Word and Sound Play

Materials: "The Rain Talks" in the Teacher's Resource Guide (page T39) and recording on CD and Theme 2 cassette

Directions: Frog likes rain sounds. Listen to "The Rain Talks." Let's say the chant. Listen for the beginning sound in **ping-ping**. Let's change that sound to **ding-ding**. Look at the picture. Put an X on three things that make a noise when the rain falls on them.

With your child, take turns making rain sounds. Drum your hands on a tabletop, pie tin, or plastic container. Talk about different sounds you make.

Home Activity

26

© William H. Sadlier, Inc. All rights reserved.

Time to Listen

Purpose: Listening Comprehension—Following Directions
Materials: "What Will Ana Wear?" in the Teacher's Resource Guide (page T39) and recording on CD and Theme 2 cassette
Directions: Look at the pictures. Listen to a story about Ana to find out what she wears today. Now listen carefully and follow my directions. Circle the bathing suit. Put an X on the sandals. Draw a line under the sunglasses.

27

Purposes: Science—Comparing Objects; Oral Language Development—Communicating Observations

Directions: Let's talk about the wind. The wind can move a kite. What else can the wind move? Look at the pictures and name them with me. You will use this page to see if the wind can move these things. (See page 28 in the Teacher's Resource Guide for the Science Center activity.)

28

Activity 21

Ask your child to tell you what happened when he or she blew on each item pictured above.

© William H. Sadlier, Inc. All rights reserved.

Purpose: Visual Discrimination—Patterning with Colors

Directions: Let's name the pictures together. Now let's look at the colors in each row. In the first row I see red-yellow-red-yellow. These colors make a pattern. Color the last picture in each row to keep the color patterns going.

29

Let's make a shape pattern.

Let's make another pattern.

Purpose: Visual Discrimination—Patterning with Shapes
Materials: Punchout Cards on page 75
Directions: Let's look at the shapes in each row. I see a square-circle-square-circle. These shapes make a pattern. Let's use our cards to make this pattern. Now let's use our cards to make the pattern in the last row.

30

Activity 23

Home
Activity

Cut two diamond and two oval shapes out of paper. Help your child use the shapes to make a pattern.

© William H. Sadlier, Inc. All rights reserved.

Purpose: Learning About the Alphabet—Recognizing Uppercase Letters

Materials: "The Weather Alphabet Song" in the Teacher's Resource Guide (page T39) and recording on CD and Theme 2 cassette

Directions: Point to each letter in the alphabet as I say its name. Now sing "The Weather Alphabet Song" with me. Circle the first letter in your last name.

31

Activity 24

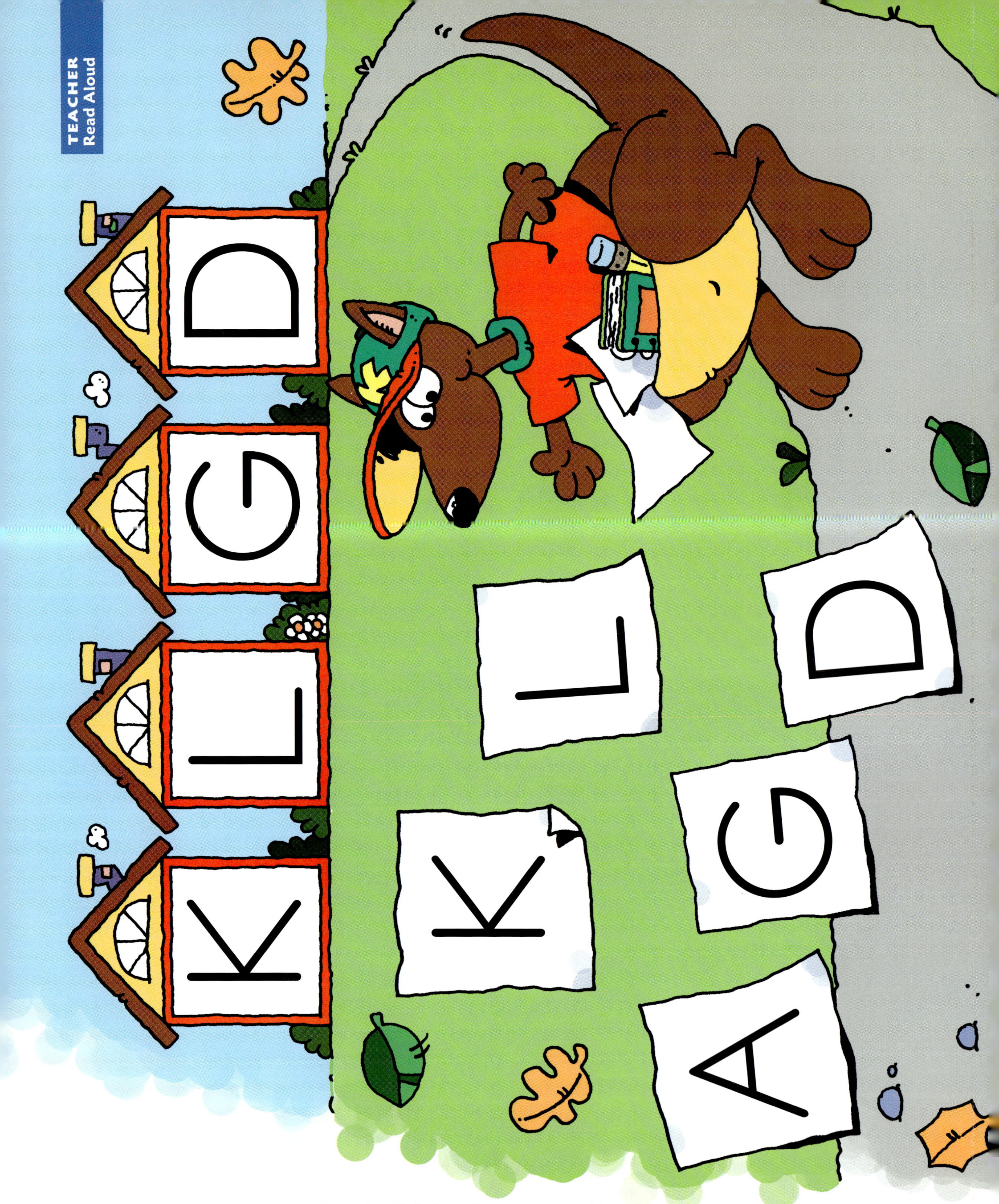

Purpose: Learning About the Alphabet—Recognizing and Matching Uppercase Letters

Directions: The wind is blowing Kelly Kangaroo's papers. Listen as I say a letter name. Point to the letter on the house with me. Then circle the same letter on one of Kelly's papers.

Name the letter on each house. Have your child point to each letter and say its name.

Tickets

Popcorn

75¢

Rides

© William H. Sadlier, Inc. All rights reserved.

Purpose: Learning About Print—Understanding that Messages Come from Print
Directions: Look at the picture. The words on the signs tell us where to find things in the amusement park. I'm pointing to the sign that says "Tickets." Color this sign blue. Now I'm pointing to the sign that says "Popcorn." Color this sign red. The last sign says "Rides." Color this sign green.

My Own Word Cards

rain

wind

snow

hat

boots

umbrella

34

Activity 27

Purposes: Learning About Print—Recognizing Words; Sight Vocabulary—Theme Words
Directions: Let's talk about the pictures. What do you see? Listen as I read one of the words. Hold up the card with the picture and word I say.

Look and Learn

Let's build a snowman.

Eyes

Nose

Mouth

Buttons

© William H. Sadlier, Inc. All rights reserved.

Think and Share

What are some parts of the snowman's body?
What things can you use to make each part?

Purpose: Comprehension—Recalling Details
Directions: Find out how to build a snowman. Point to each picture as I read about it.

35

Activity 28

36

Activity 29

Purpose: Writing—Sharing Ideas Through Drawing and Writing
Directions: Sometimes a rainy day keeps us inside. Draw or write about what you like to do indoors on rainy days.

Home Activity

Ask your child to tell you about the drawing or writing on this page. Make a plan of something you can do together when it rains.

Sun Fun

© William H. Sadlier, Inc. All rights reserved.

Fold

Directions: Have your child show you the front and back of this book. Before reading the book to your child, look at the pictures. Ask your child to tell about the places shown in the photos. Then read the story aloud.

Parent Read Aloud

Families swim.

Families eat.

4

TAKE-HOME BOOK
Book Concepts: Identifying Parts of a Book; Differentiating Between Pictures and Print
Comprehension: Identifying the Setting

Activity 30

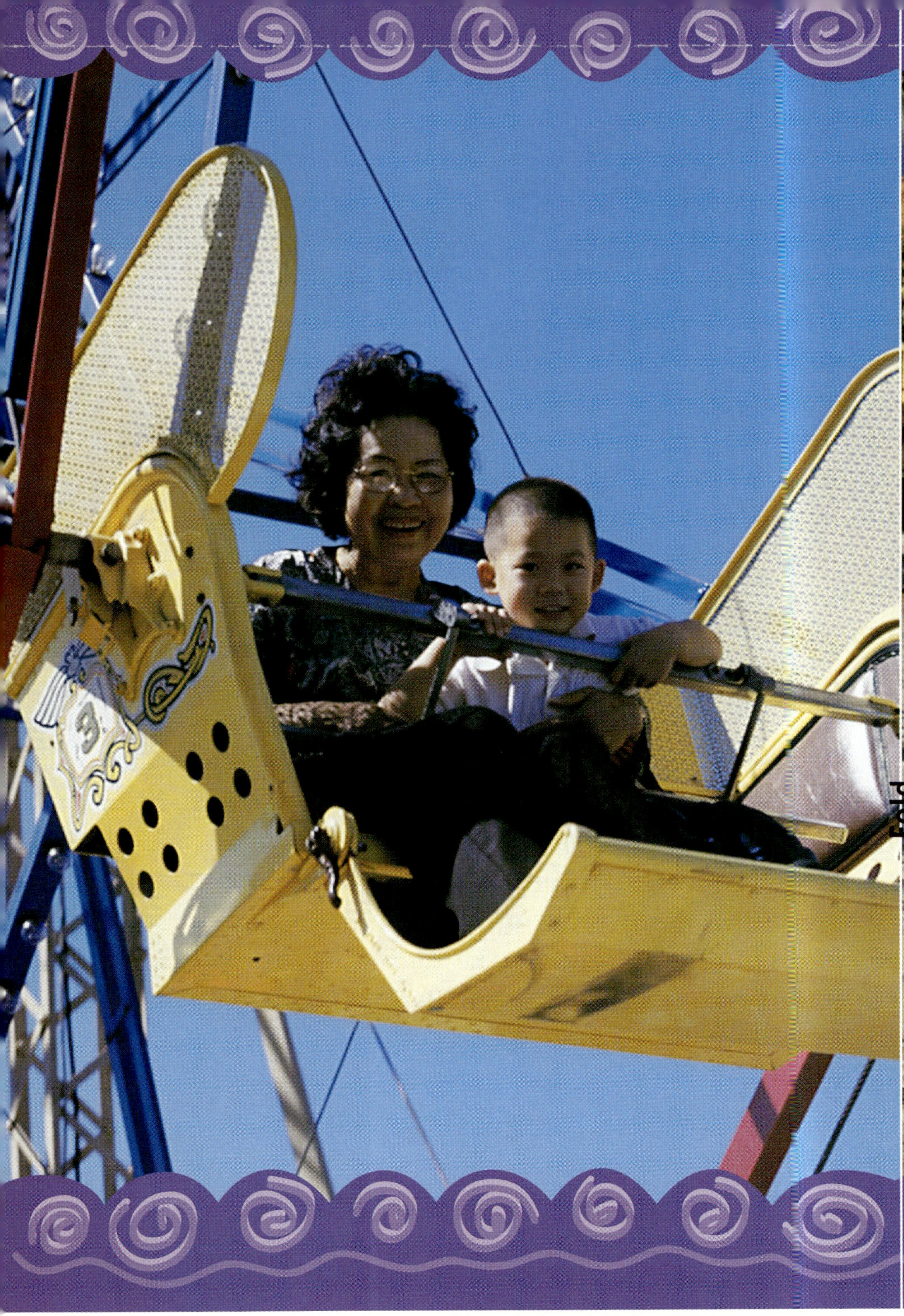

2

Families ride.

Fold

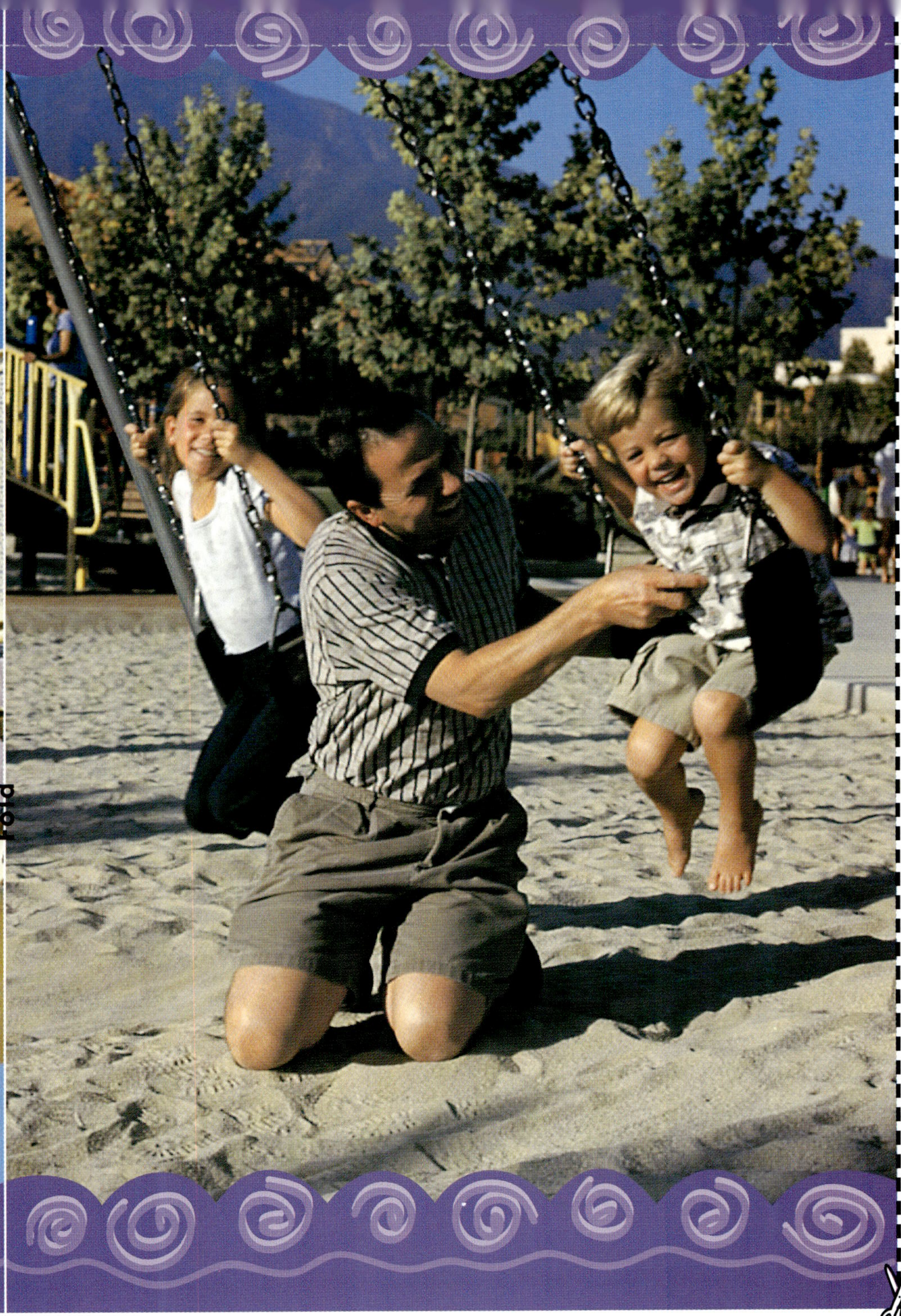

Families swing.

3

TAKE-HOME BOOK
Book Concepts: Identifying Parts of a Book; Differentiating Between Pictures and Print
Comprehension: Identifying the Setting

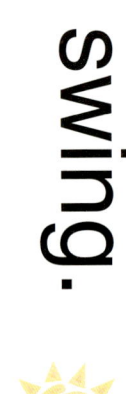

The Itsy Bitsy Spider

The itsy bitsy spider
climbed up the water spout.
Down came the rain and
washed the spider out.
Out came the sun and
dried up all the rain,
And the itsy bitsy spider
climbed up the spout again.

Think and Share
What are some other things spiders can do besides climb?

Purposes: Phonemic Awareness—Rhyme; Reading Behavior—Responding to Text
Directions: Look at the picture as I read the rhyme aloud. Now look at the words as I read the rhyme aloud.

© William H. Sadlier, Inc. All rights reserved.

Dear Family,

Read the rhyme "The Itsy Bitsy Spider" on the reverse side of this page to your child. Talk to your child about spiders. What do they look like? How do they move?

Directions: Teach your child the rhyme below. Follow the drawings in each box to help your child act out each line as you read the rhyme.

Apreciada Familia:

Lea al niño la rima "The Itsy Bitsy Spider" en la página 39. Hablen sobre las arañas. ¿Cuál es su aspecto? ¿Cómo se mueven?

Indicaciones: Enseñe al niño la rima escrita abajo. Mientras usted lee el poema, siga la indicación en cada cuadro para ayudar al niño a escenificar cada línea.

Home Activity

Stop!

And look. Oh, what a show!

Ants are marching in a row,

Spiders climbing very slow,

Bees flying high and low,

To tiny friends, wave "Hello!"

40

Activity 31

Purpose: Oral Language Development—Dramatizing and Retelling a Rhyme

Visit us at
www.sadlier-oxford.com

© William H. Sadlier, Inc. All rights reserved.

Time to Talk

Purpose: Oral Language Development—Using Descriptive Language
Directions: Look at the picture. I see a blue and purple butterfly. What do you see?
Talk about all of the insects you see. Use many different words to tell about each insect.

41

Activity 32

Tug, bug, tug!   Tug the rug!

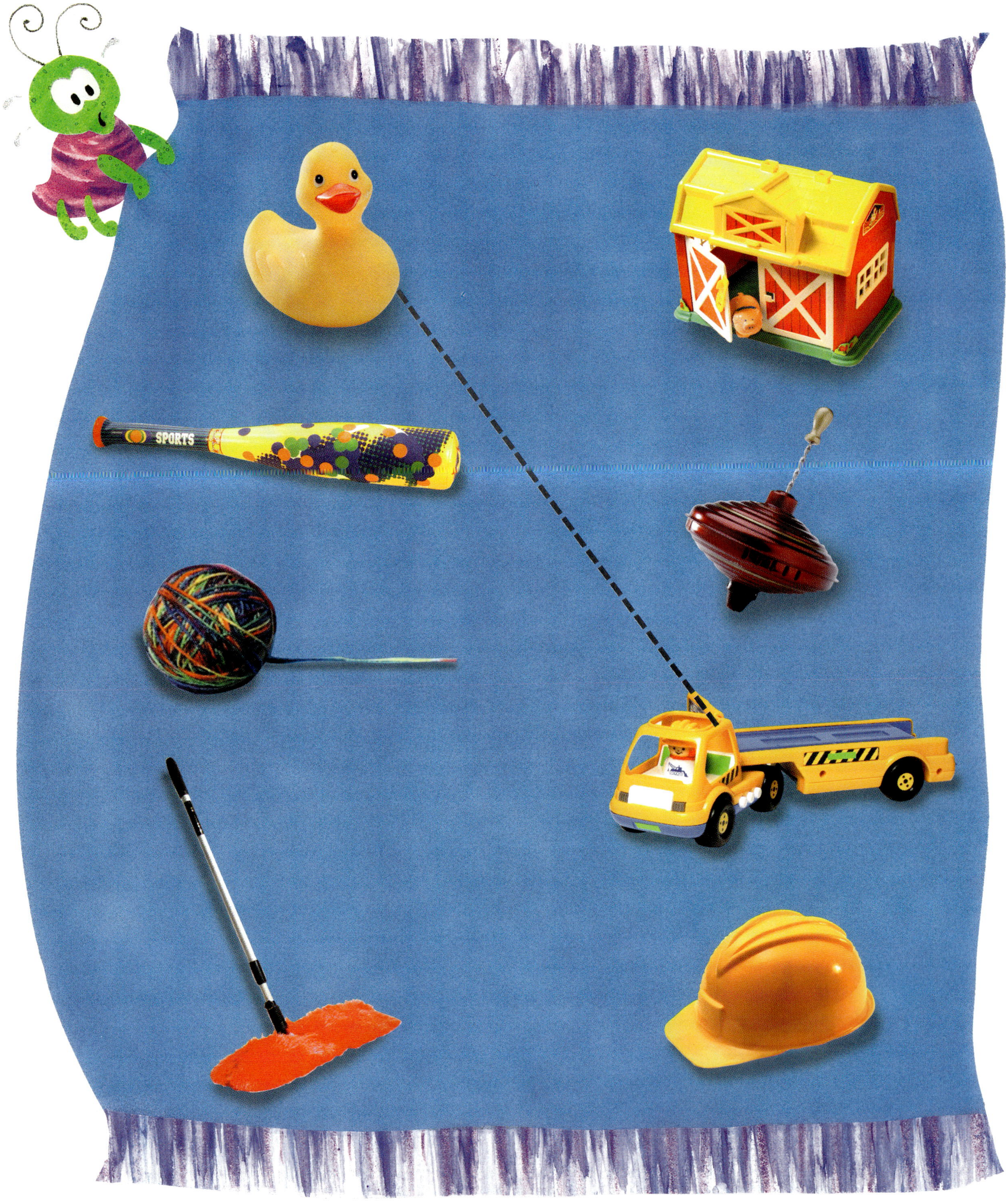

Purpose: Phonemic Awareness and Auditory Discrimination—Rhyme
Directions: Tug and **bug** rhyme. Say the name of a picture on one side of the rug. Find a picture name that rhymes on the other side of the rug. Draw a line to connect the pictures that have rhyming names.

Home Activity

Say pairs of words such as **duck** and **truck**. Have your child clap if the words rhyme.

© William H. Sadlier, Inc. All rights reserved.

Purpose: Listening Comprehension—Responding to Questions

Materials: "Ride and Slide Rhymes" in the Teacher's Resource Guide (page T40) and recording on CD and Theme 3 cassette

Directions: Listen to each rhyme. Answer each question I ask. Then draw a line from each bug to show where it plays.

43

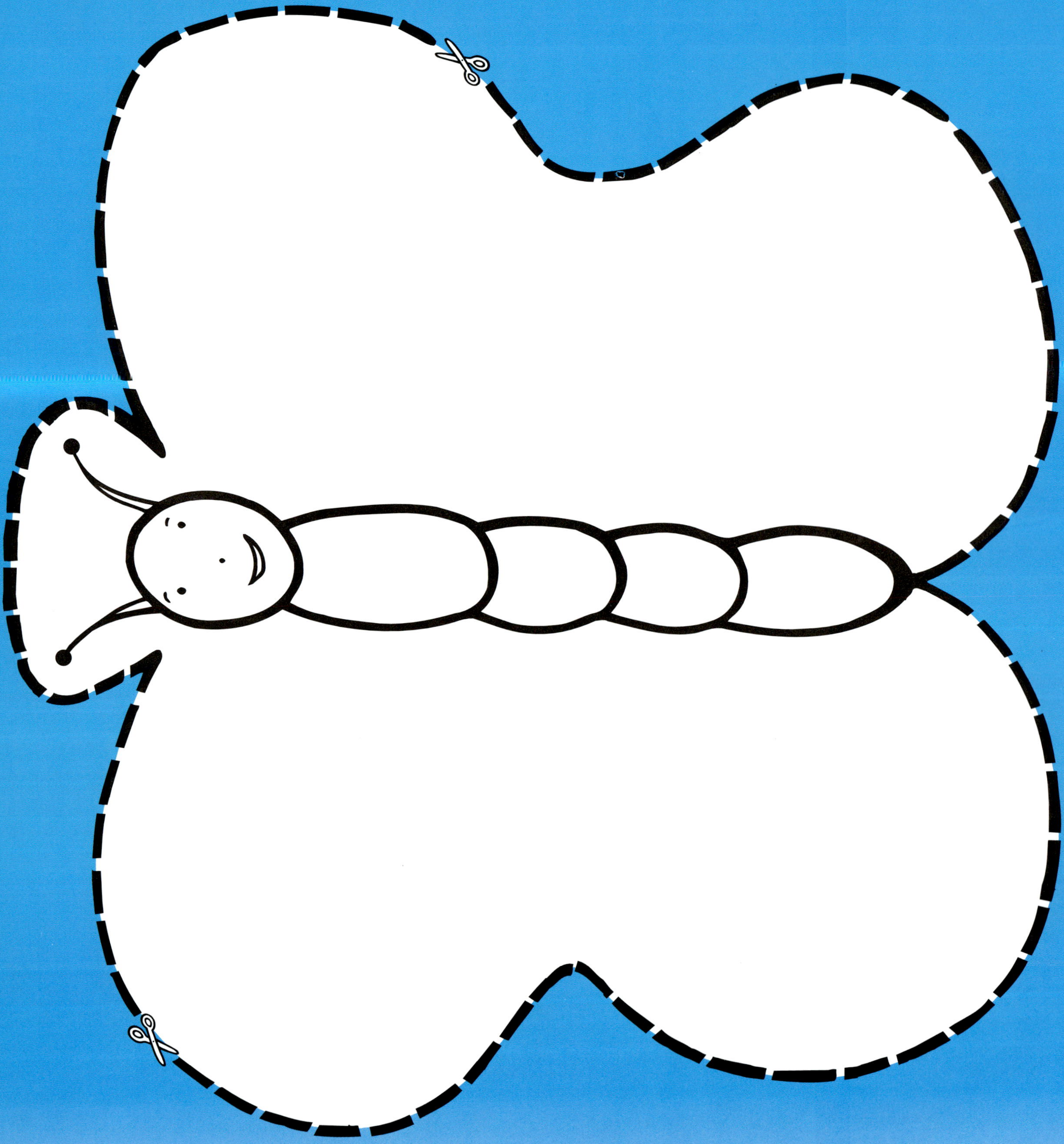

44

Activity 35

Purposes: Art—Completing a Picture; Oral Language Development—Telling a Story
Directions: Cut out the butterfly. Crumple little pieces of colored tissue paper and glue them on the butterfly. Then tell a story about your butterfly.

© William H. Sadlier, Inc. All rights reserved.

Purpose: Visual Discrimination—Classifying

Directions: Lulu Bug is looking for some new things to wear. Help her shop at the yard sale. Look at all of the things for sale. Circle each item that Lulu could wear.

45

Activity 36

Nibble, nibble, munch.
Ants love a picnic lunch.

Purpose: Visual Discrimination—Classifying
Materials: Punchout Cards on page 77
Directions: Listen as I read the rhyme aloud. Now help pack the picnic basket. Look at each card. If the picture shows something you might eat at a picnic, place the card in the basket.

46

Activity 37

Home Activity

Name different foods or objects. Ask your child whether he or she would bring them on a picnic.

© William H. Sadlier, Inc. All rights reserved.

a b c d e f g

h i j k l m n

o p q r s t u

v w x y z

Purpose: Learning About the Alphabet—Recognizing Lowercase Letters
Materials: "The Bugs Alphabet Song" in the Teacher's Resource Guide (page T40)
and recording on CD and Theme 3 cassette
Directions: Point to each letter in the alphabet as I say its name. Now sing "The Bugs
Alphabet Song" with me. Circle a letter that is in your name.

47

w

c

c

d

j

d

n

b

k

r

u

r

48

Activity 39

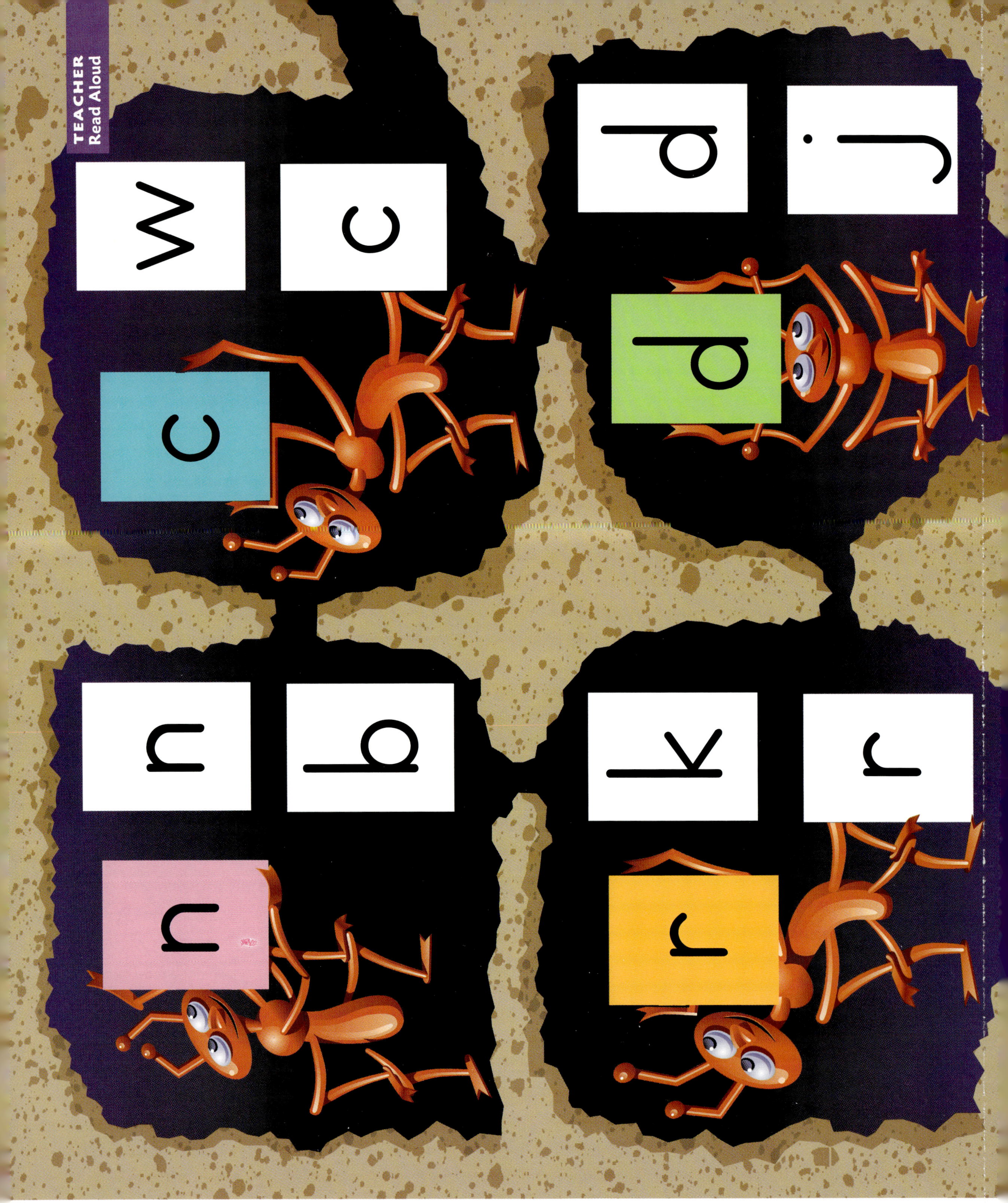

Purpose: Learning About the Alphabet—Recognizing and Matching
Lowercase Letters

Directions: Listen as I name the letter that each ant is holding.
Point to the letter. Say its name with me. Find the same letter next
to the ant and color the box.

Home Activity

Point to the letter in
each box. Say the letter
name and have your
child repeat it after you.

Can you find the words in this garden?

Lettuce

Pumpkin

Corn

Tomato

© William H. Sadlier, Inc. All rights reserved.

Purpose: Learning About Print—Understanding the Concept of a Word
Directions: Talk about what you see in this garden. Find and circle four words. Listen as I read the words aloud. Then find the itsy bitsy spider.

49

My Own Word Cards

spider

ant

butterfly

ladybug

bee

grasshopper

50

Activity 41

Purposes: Learning About Print—Recognizing Words; Sight Vocabulary—Theme Words
Directions: Let's talk about the pictures. What do you see? Listen as I read one of the words. Hold up the card with the picture and word I say.

Look
and
Learn

Look at all the bugs.

small

strong

© William H. Sadlier, Inc. All rights reserved.

tall

long

Think and Share
How are the bugs the same?
How are the bugs different?

Purpose: Comprehension—Making Comparisons
Directions: Point to each picture as I read about it.
Now let's talk about all the bugs.

51

Activity 42

Beginning to Write

52

Activity 43

Purpose: Writing—Sharing Ideas Through Drawing and Writing
Directions: Be a bug detective. Look very closely at a bug you see outside or pictured in this book. Then draw or write about the bug.

Ask your child to tell you about the bug he or she drew or wrote about.

Home Activity

Bugs

Directions: Read the story with your child. Have your child look at each picture and then point to each word as you read. Talk about the colors of the bugs. Help your child name other things that are these colors.

A yellow bug.

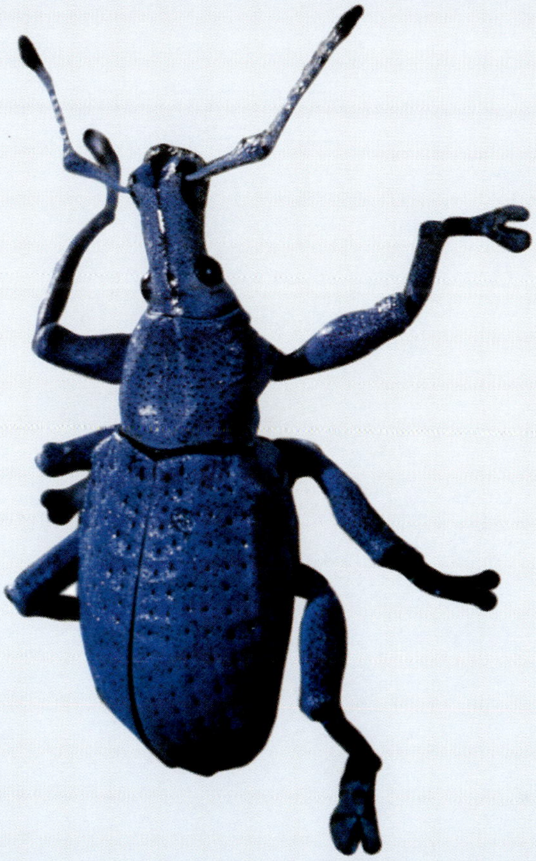

A blue bug!

© William H. Sadlier, Inc. All rights reserved.

TAKE-HOME BOOK
Book Concepts: Recognizing that Both Print and Pictures Convey Meaning; Knowing that Print and Pictures on a Page Are Related
Comprehension: Classifying

2

A red bug.

Fold

A green bug.

3

TAKE-HOME BOOK
Book Concepts: Recognizing that Both Print and Pictures Convey Meaning;
Knowing that Print and Pictures on a Page Are Related
Comprehension: Classifying

© William H. Sadlier, Inc. All rights reserved.

TEACHER Read Aloud

THEME Let's Pretend

Hey Diddle, Diddle

Hey diddle, diddle,

The cat and the fiddle,

The cow jumped over

the moon;

The little dog laughed

To see such sport,

And the dish ran away

with the spoon.

Think and Share

What makes this poem silly?

Purposes: Phonemic Awareness—Rhyme; Reading Behavior—Responding to Text
Directions: Look at the picture as I read the rhyme aloud. Now look at the words as I read the rhyme aloud.

Home
Activity

Dear Family,

Read the rhyme "Hey Diddle, Diddle" on the reverse side of this page to your child. Recite together any other nursery rhymes that you know.

Directions: Teach your child one of the rhymes below. Let your child suggest names of family members, such as Grandma, to complete the lines. Read the rhyme again and again, using the names chosen. Then repeat with the second rhyme.

Apreciada Familia:

Lea al niño la rima "Hey Diddle, Diddle" en la página 55. Reciten juntos cualquier verso que sepan.

Indicaciones: Enseñe a su hijo una de las rimas que se encuentran abajo. Permita al niño sugerir nombres de familiares por ejemplo Grandma, para completar los versos. Lea la rima una y otra vez usando los nombres escogidos. Después haga lo mismo con la segunda estrofa.

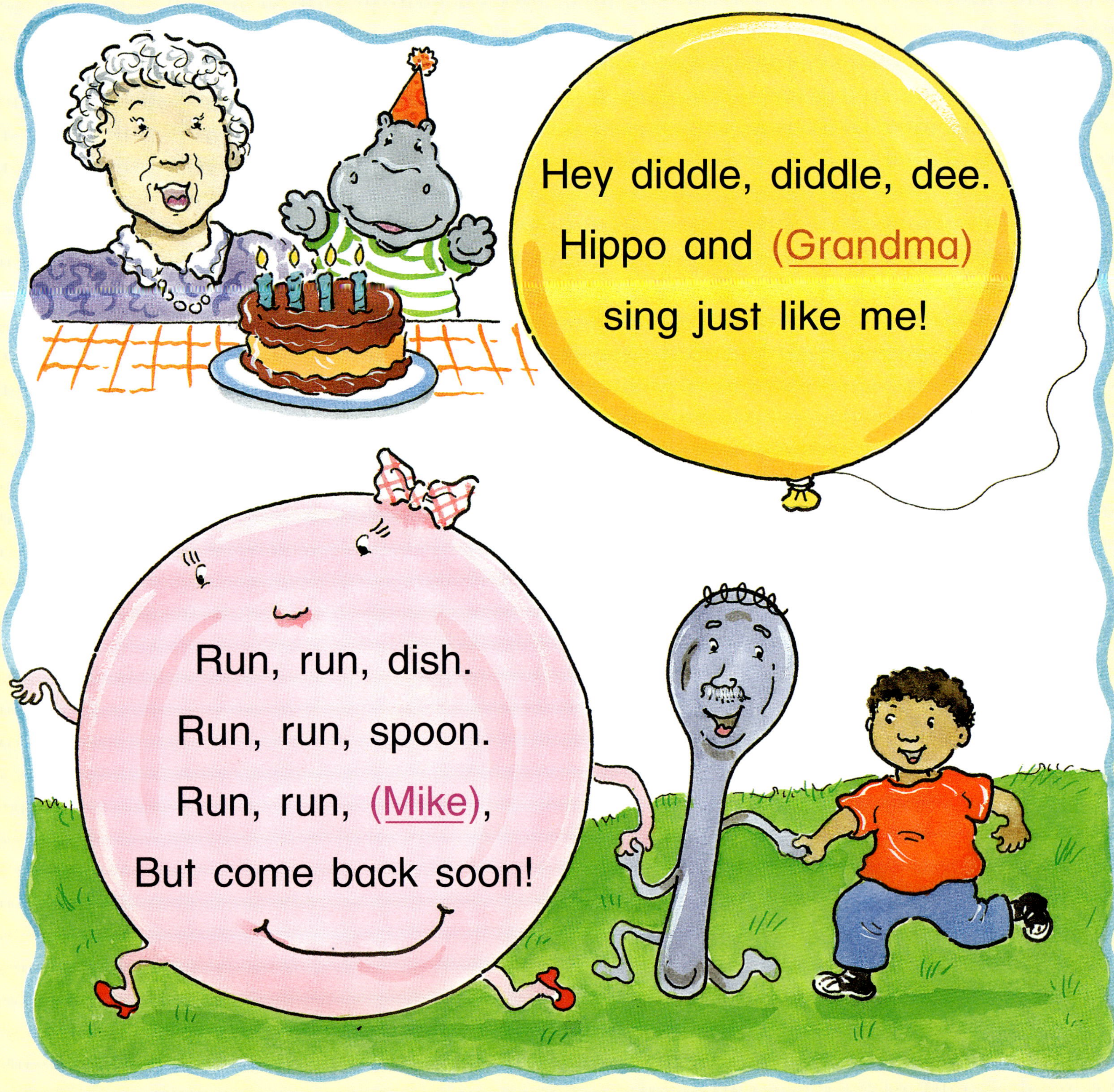
Hey diddle, diddle, dee.
Hippo and (Grandma)
sing just like me!
Run, run, dish.
Run, run, spoon.
Run, run, (Mike),
But come back soon!

Purpose: Oral Language Development—Reciting Nursery Rhymes

Internet
Visit us at
www.sadlier-oxford.com

© William H. Sadlier, Inc. All rights reserved.

Purpose: Oral Language Development—Retelling a Story

Materials: "Megan's Mixed-Up Day" in the Teacher's Resource Guide (page T41) and recording on CD and Theme 4 cassette

Directions: Look at the pictures. Listen to what happened to Megan one mixed-up day. Now use the pictures to tell the story of Megan's mixed-up day in your own words.

57

Purpose: Phonemic Awareness and Auditory Discrimination—
Alliteration

Materials: "Higglety, Higglety, Hop Rhymes" in the Teacher's Resource
Guide (page T41) and recording on CD and Theme 4 cassette

Directions: Listen to the rhymes. Put an X on the animal with a
name that begins like **higglety, higglety, hop**. Draw a box around the
animal with a name that begins like **pigglety, pigglety, pop**. Circle
the animal with a name that begins like **digglety, digglety, dop**.

With your child, take turns
saying real and nonsense
words that have the
same beginning sound
as **higglety, higglety, hop**.

58

© William H. Sadlier, Inc. All rights reserved.

Time
to
Listen

Purpose: Listening Comprehension—Responding to Simple Commands
Materials: "Look in the Mirror" in the Teacher's Resource Guide (page T41) and recording on CD and Theme 4 cassette
Directions: Look at the picture. Listen as I read about the boy in the mirror. Now listen again and do each thing to the picture that I say. Color the boy's hair green. Put spots on the boy's tie. Color the boy's cat purple.

59

Activity 48

60

Purposes: Dramatic Play—Participating in Creative Play; Building Vocabulary—Naming Animals
Directions: Look at the animal cards. What animals do you see? Point to the bottom of the zebra. Cut out all of the cards. Now you're going to use your cards to pretend you are a make-believe animal. (See page 60 in the Teacher's Resource Guide for the Dramatic Play Center activity.)

© William H. Sadlier, Inc. All rights reserved.

Purpose: Visual Discrimination—Something's Wrong
Materials: Punchout Cards on page 79
Directions: There is something wrong with three of the toys in this toy store that makes them look funny. Circle each thing that is wrong. Now look at your cards. There is something wrong with four of these toys that makes them look funny too. Put all of the funny toys in the toy store.

61

Purpose: Visual Discrimination—Something's Missing
Directions: Look at the animals in the band. Circle the animal in each row that is missing something.

Home Activity

Draw two flowers that are the same, except one is missing its stem. Ask your child to tell and draw what is missing.

Aa Bb Cc Dd Ee

Ff Gg Hh Ii Jj Kk

Ll Mm Nn Oo Pp

Qq Rr Ss Tt Uu

Vv Ww Xx Yy Zz

© William H. Sadlier, Inc. All rights reserved.

Purpose: Learning About the Alphabet—Recognizing Uppercase and Lowercase Letters

Materials: "The Let's Pretend Alphabet Song" in the Teacher's Resource Guide (page T41) and recording on CD and Theme 4 cassette

Directions: Point to each pair of letters as I say their names. These uppercase and lowercase letters are called partner letters. Now sing "The Let's Pretend Alphabet Song" with me. I will circle all of the partner letters that you can name.

63

Activity 52

p

h

m

H

M

P

Purpose: Learning About the Alphabet—Recognizing and Matching Uppercase and Lowercase Letters

Directions: Listen as I say a letter name. Point to the uppercase letter on the balloon with me and say its name. Color the balloon. Now find a balloon with the partner letter. Color this balloon the same color. Use a different color for each pair of partner letters.

64

Activity 53

Home Activity

Write partner letters such as **Bb**, **Ff**, and **Rr** on a piece of paper. Have your child point to each pair of letters as you say their names.

Letters make up words.

© William H. Sadlier, Inc. All rights reserved.

Purpose: *Learning About Print—Understanding that Letters Make Up Words*
Directions: Point to the letters **c-a-t** with me. Let's count these letters on our fingers. These three letters make up one word. Point to the word **cat** with me. Now point to the letters **f-r-o-g** with me. Let's count these letters on our fingers. These four letters make up one word. Point to the word **frog** with me.

65

Activity 54

TEACHER Read Aloud

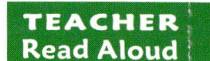

My Own Word Cards

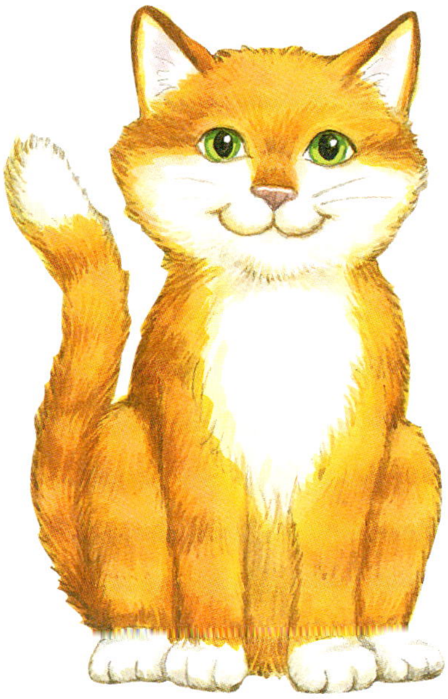

cat

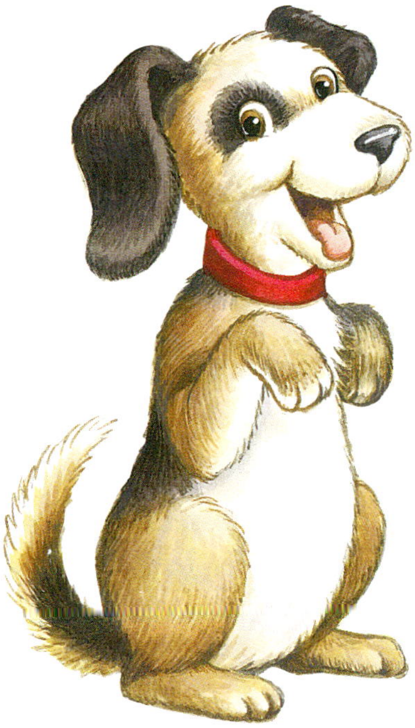

dog

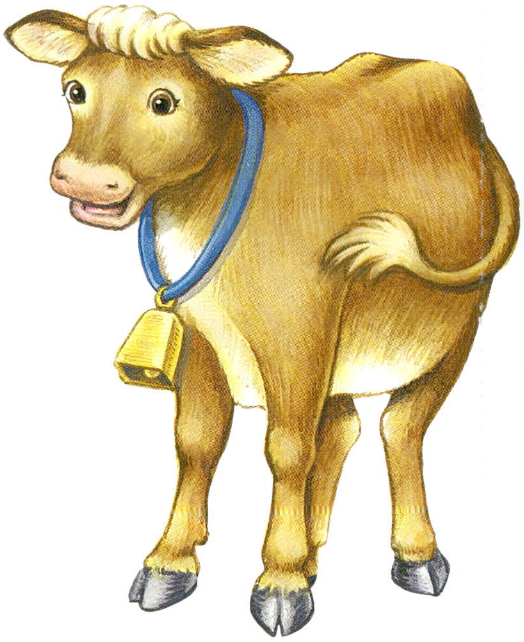

cow

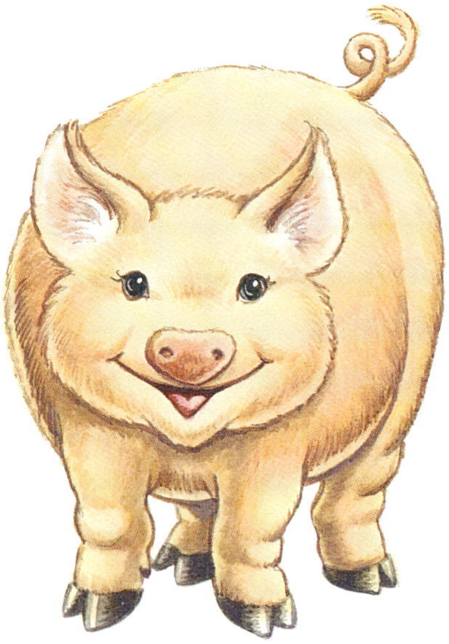

pig

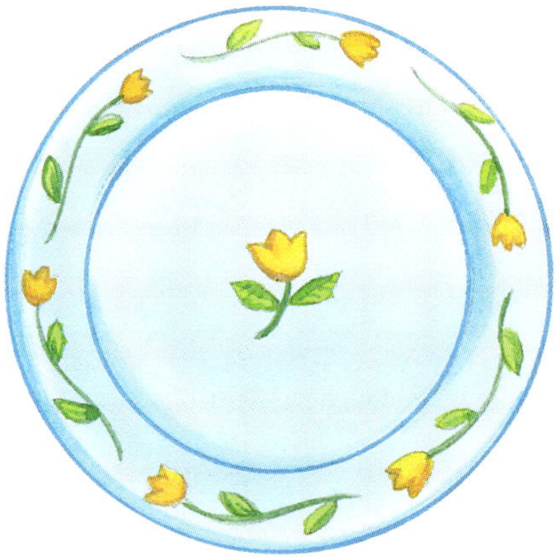

dish

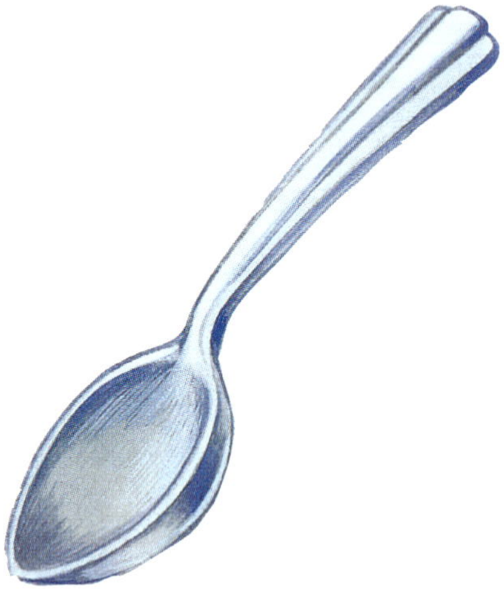

spoon

Purposes: Learning About Print—Recognizing Words; Sight Vocabulary—Theme Words

Directions: Let's talk about the pictures. What do you see? Listen as I read one of the words. Hold up the card with the picture and word I say.

The circus is coming!

Look and Learn

clowns

popcorn

tigers

tricks

© William H. Sadlier, Inc. All rights reserved.

Think and Share

Would it be fun to see a real circus? Tell why.
Where else could you see the things in these pictures?

Purpose: Comprehension—Drawing Conclusions
Directions: Find out what you would see at the circus.
Point to each picture as I read about it.

Beginning to Write

Purpose: Writing—Sharing Ideas Through Drawing and Writing

Directions: Listen as I read part of a silly story to you: Today was the funniest day ever. I went outside to play. When I looked up in the sky, I saw a _____. Think of something funny you might see up in the sky. Draw or write your answer in the cloud.

Home Activity

Help your child draw or write about something that you might really see in the sky.

A Silly School

Directions: Before reading this book, look at the pictures with your child. Ask if he or she thinks the story is real or make-believe and why. Then read the story aloud to your child. Have your child move a finger from left to right below each sentence as you read it.

Parent Read Aloud

Fold

Rabbits are reading.

1

Cats are clapping.

4

TAKE-HOME BOOK
Book Concepts: Tracking Print from Left to Right;
Understanding that Print Represents Spoken Language
Comprehension: Distinguishing Fantasy/Reality

69

Activity 58

2

Pigs are painting.

Fold

3

Bears are building.

TAKE-HOME BOOK
Book Concepts: Tracking Print from Left to Right;
Understanding that Print Represents Spoken Language
Comprehension: Distinguishing Fantasy/Reality

Name _____ Year 20_____-20 _____

Literacy Development Checklist

A Always **S** Sometimes **N** Never

Beginning Literacy Skills

Phonemic Awareness and Auditory Discrimination

☐ Identifies Rhyme: pp. 5, 23, 39, 42, 55
☐ Recognizes Environmental Sounds: p. 8
☐ Demonstrates Word and Sound Play: p. 26
☐ Recognizes Alliteration: p. 58

Oral Language Development

☐ Communicates Personal Experiences: p. 6
☐ Builds Vocabulary: pp. 7, 10, 18, 34, 50, 60, 66
☐ Asks Questions: p. 24
☐ Speaks in Complete Sentences: p. 25
☐ Communicates Observations: p. 28
☐ Dramatizes and Retells a Rhyme: p. 40
☐ Uses Descriptive Language: p. 41
☐ Tells a Story: p. 44
☐ Recites Nursery Rhymes: pp. 5, 23, 39, 55, 56
☐ Retells a Story: pp. 21–22, 57

Listening Comprehension

☐ Recalls Details: p. 9
☐ Follows Directions: p. 27
☐ Responds to Questions: p. 43
☐ Responds to Simple Commands: p. 59

Visual Discrimination

☐ Recognizes Same/Different: pp. 11–12
☐ Patterns with Colors: p. 29
☐ Patterns with Shapes: p. 30
☐ Classifies Objects: pp. 45–46
☐ Identifies Something's Wrong: p. 61
☐ Identifies Something's Missing: p. 62

Date and Teacher Observations

Copyright © by William H. Sadlier, Inc.

71

Beginning Literacy Skills

The Alphabet

- ❑ Recognizes and Matches Uppercase Letters: pp. 13–14, 31–32
- ❑ Recognizes and Matches Lowercase Letters: pp. 47–48
- ❑ Recognizes and Matches Uppercase and Lowercase Letters: pp. 63–64

Beginning Print Concepts

- ❑ Demonstrates Left-to-Right Progression: p. 15
- ❑ Demonstrates Top-to-Bottom Progression: p. 16
- ❑ Recognizes One's First Name: p. 17
- ❑ Develops Sight Vocabulary: pp. 18, 34, 50, 66
- ❑ Understands that Messages Come from Print: p. 33
- ❑ Understands the Concept of a Word: p. 49
- ❑ Understands that Letters Make Up Words: p. 65

Comprehension Skills

- ❑ Sequences: p. 19
- ❑ Retells a Story: pp. 21–22, 57
- ❑ Recalls Details: p. 35
- ❑ Identifies the Setting: pp. 37–38
- ❑ Makes Comparisons: p. 51
- ❑ Classifies Objects: pp. 53–54
- ❑ Draws Conclusions: p. 67
- ❑ Distinguishes Fantasy/Reality: pp. 69–70

Beginning Writing

- ❑ Shares Ideas Through Drawing and Writing: pp. 20, 36, 52, 68

Beginning Book Concepts

- ❑ Knows How to Hold a Book Upright: pp. 21–22
- ❑ Knows How to Turn Pages Properly: pp. 21–22
- ❑ Identifies Parts of a Book: pp. 37–38
- ❑ Differentiates Between Pictures and Print: pp. 37–38
- ❑ Recognizes that Both Print and Pictures Convey Meaning: pp. 53–54
- ❑ Knows that Print and Pictures on a Page Are Related: pp. 53–54
- ❑ Tracks Print from Left to Right: pp. 69–70
- ❑ Understands that Print Represents Spoken Language: pp. 69–70

72

Permission to duplicate this checklist for classroom use is granted to users of *Getting Ready to Read with Mother Goose* by William H. Sadlier, Inc.